Date: 2/27/12

J BIO BIRD
Boone, Mary,
Sue Bird /

D1088576

SUE
BIRD

Mary Boone

Mitchell Lane
PUBLISHERS

P.O. Box 196
Hockessin, Delaware 19707
Visit us on the web: www.mitchelllane.com
Comments? email us: mitchelllane@mitchelllane.com

Mitchell Lane
PUBLISHERS

Copyright © 2012 by Mitchell Lane Publishers. All rights reserved. No part of this book may be reproduced without written permission from the publisher. Printed and bound in the United States of America.

Printing   1   2   3   4   5   6   7   8   9

A Robbie Reader Biography

Abigail Breslin	Dr. Seuss	Mia Hamm
Adrian Peterson	Dwayne "The Rock" Johnson	Miley Cyrus
Albert Einstein	Dwyane Wade	Miranda Cosgrove
Albert Pujols	Dylan & Cole Sprouse	Philo Farnsworth
Alex Rodriguez	Eli Manning	Raven-Symoné
Aly and AJ	Emily Osment	Roy Halladay
AnnaSophia Robb	Emma Watson	Selena Gomez
Amanda Bynes	Hilary Duff	Shaquille O'Neal
Ashley Tisdale	Jaden Smith	Story of Harley-Davidson
Brenda Song	Jamie Lynn Spears	**Sue Bird**
Brittany Murphy	Jennette McCurdy	Syd Hoff
Charles Schulz	Jesse McCartney	Taylor Lautner
Chris Johnson	Jimmie Johnson	Tiki Barber
Cliff Lee	Johnny Gruelle	Tim Lincecum
Dakota Fanning	Jonas Brothers	Tom Brady
Dale Earnhardt Jr.	Jordin Sparks	Tony Hawk
David Archuleta	Justin Beiber	Troy Polamalu
Demi Lovato	Keke Palmer	Victoria Justice
Donovan McNabb	Larry Fitzgerald	
Drake Bell & Josh Peck	LeBron James	

Library of Congress Cataloging-in-Publication Data
Boone, Mary, 1963–
Sue Bird / by Mary Boone.
    p. cm. — (A Robbie reader)
Includes bibliographical references and index.
ISBN 978-1-61228-062-2 (library bound)
1. Bird, Sue—Juvenile literature. 2. Women basketball players—United States—Biography—Juvenile literature. I. Title.
GV884.B572B66 2012
796.323082—dc23
                                       2011016788

eBook ISBN: 9781612281742

ABOUT THE AUTHOR: Mary Boone has written more than 20 books for young readers, including Robbie Reader Biographies about baseball player David Wright and actress Jennette McCurdy. Mary, her husband Mitch, and her kids, Eve and Eli, live in Tacoma, Washington, and proudly cheer for Sue Bird and her Seattle Storm teammates.

PUBLISHER'S NOTE: The following story has been thoroughly researched and to the best of our knowledge represents a true story. While every possible effort has been made to ensure accuracy, the publisher will not assume liability for damages caused by inaccuracies in the data, and makes no warranty on the accuracy of the information contained herein. This story has not been authorized or endorsed by Sue Bird.

TABLE OF CONTENTS

Words in **bold** type can be found in the glossary.

Sue Bird has been a leader in women's basketball since her days at the University of Connecticut (UConn).

A Desire to Win

Sue Bird was angrier than she'd ever been on the basketball court. Her University of Connecticut team was the best in women's college basketball. They went to South Bend, Indiana, assuming Notre Dame was the same old team they had defeated the past three seasons. "Assuming" cost them the game.

"A lot of us were like, 'Oh yeah, this is Notre Dame, we've beaten them for eight years and, well, we are UConn, and we are gonna win,' " she told the *Daily News*.

Notre Dame outscored Bird and her teammates by 15 points.

Bird says her team was beaten because their **opponent** (uh-POH-nunt) was better prepared. Notre Dame fought for the win—and got it.

That loss in January 2001 was a turning point for Bird. She became more direct, saying she was embarrassed (em-BAH-rusd) by her team's lack of effort. She became a more demanding leader, pushing her teammates to do better. She stopped worrying about messing up. A new, stronger Sue Bird emerged.

She has since become one of the best-known players in the Women's National Basketball Association (WNBA). At 5 feet 9 inches tall, Bird is one of the Seattle Storm's best scorers, **defenders**, and **rebounders**. Her teams have earned two **NCAA** Division I national championships (CHAM-pee-un-ships), two WNBA championships, and two Olympic gold medals.

If she sounds like she's serious, she is— on the court. When the final buzzer sounds, though, Bird is a fun-loving prankster. She likes to watch movies and shoot pool with her teammates and pals. She happily poses for photos and chats with fans. In 2010, more

Bird, shown with Seattle Storm teammate Lauren Jackson (right), has become one of the stars of women's professional basketball.

than 400,000 people voted for her as the Northwest's Friendliest Professional Athlete. Sportswriters agree: She is both charming and modest.

Bird and fellow Storm star Lauren Jackson are close friends and longtime roommates. "If I need to **confide** in anyone, she's one of the first people I talk to," Jackson told the *Los Angeles Times*. "She's on the same page with me on the court and off the court. It's great."

As a child, Sue was good at most of the sports she tried. She was nice and respectful, but always played to win.

A Tomboy

Suzanne Brigit Bird was born October 16, 1980, to Herschel and Nancy Bird. Her older sister, Jen, played on a basketball team, and Sue wanted to be just like her. Sue has always been **competitive** (kum-PEH-tih-tiv), whether she is playing board games with her family or soccer at a local park.

"You could say I was **hardwired** [HARD-wyrd] to be competitive," she wrote in her 2004 biography. "I loved doing everything the boys in my neighborhood liked to do—ride bikes, play whatever sport was in season at the nearby park, or climb trees. I was a tomboy."

When Sue was in sixth grade, she started playing **AAU** basketball. She attended Syosset (sy-AH-set) High School for her freshman (first) and sophomore (second) years, and played as a point guard on that school's basketball team. Point guards are on-the-floor leaders who run the team's offense. They make sure the ball gets to the right player at the right time. It was a position that suited Sue.

In the mid-1990s, Bird attended an **exhibition** (ek-seh-BIH-shun) game between the United States National Women's Team and China. She watched as stars including Teresa Edwards and Rebecca Lobo scored basket after basket. These U.S. athletes, known as the Women's Dream Team, won every game they played on their way to winning a gold medal at the 1996 Atlanta Olympics.

In those bleachers, while watching some of the best athletes in the world, Bird decided she, too, wanted to play in the Olympics. "When I was watching that game, I said, 'I'd love to play for that team,' " she told the *Seattle Times*. "It became my goal."

Also around that time, her parents were getting divorced. Sue moved to Queens, New

York, with her father and started going to Christ the King Regional High School. She played basketball for the school for two seasons, and her team won every game they played during that time. During her last year of high school, her team won the New York state championship.

Bird won many awards as a high school player, including the New York State Player of the Year and the New York Daily Player of the Year. She was named a WBCA (Women's Basketball Coaches Association) All-American, and she scored 11 points in the WBCA High School All-America Game.

As successful as she was in high school, she was just beginning to shine.

Bird and Diana Taurasi have been named "Huskies of Honor," meaning they are in UConn's hall of fame. The two are good friends who love to compete with and against each other.

College Hoops

Because she was a star high school player, many college coaches wanted Bird to play for their team. She chose the University of Connecticut, or UConn (YOO-kahn). It was close to home and it had a winning **tradition** (trah-DIH-shun).

Bird's college career got off to a bad start when she suffered a knee injury eight games into her first season. She had surgery and could have given up on basketball. Instead, she spent hours in the gym, lifting weights and doing exercises that would make her leg stronger.

The hard work paid off. During her second season, she led the Huskies to a 36-1 record.

The team won both the Big East Championship and the 2000 NCAA Women's Division I Basketball Tournament.

The Huskies lost just three games during Bird's final two years of college—all of them during her junior (third-year) season. Throughout college, Bird received many awards. In 2002, she was named Kodak All-American and Associated Press First Team All-American. She also won the Wade Trophy (presented each year to the best NCAA Division I women's basketball player), the Naismith Award (given to the college basketball player of the year), and the Nancy Lieberman Award (given to the nation's top college point guard).

In order to have a winning team, you need talented players. But Bird says hard work is another important ingredient. "It starts the minute you step on campus as a freshman," she told the *Syosset Patch*. "It's not just about lifting weights or running drills. You're talking about a work ethic that you have to maintain. . . . That's what makes a lot of

Bird won many awards for her outstanding college basketball career. In 2002, she was honored as an Associated Press First Team All-American. She also won the trophy for AP Player of the Year.

Bird finished her college basketball career with 1,378 points, 585 assists and 243 steals. She and her team also won two national championships.

these UConn teams so great. Coach [Geno] Auriemma sets a standard. He sets the bar very high and expects you to get to it every single game, every single practice."

That desire to work hard and achieve has stayed with Bird. "Going into the rest of my life, in every aspect, I definitely see that coming out," she said.

Many WNBA coaches had noticed her hard work and leadership. Long before the official **draft**, sports reporters believed she would be one of the first college players chosen for the WNBA.

"Sue Bird is going to be a very good pro, the type of player that you can build the future of your team around," one WNBA coach told the *New York Daily News* in March 2002.

That coach was 100 percent correct.

WNBA President Val Ackerman presents Bird with her Seattle Storm jersey. Bird was selected Number 1 in the 2002 WNBA draft. She was the first point guard to be the top pick in the league's history.

FOUR

Achieving Her Dreams

In 2001–2002, the Seattle Storm had a horrible season, winning just 10 games and losing 22. Because of that bad record, they were allowed to choose first in the WNBA draft. It was the second year in a row they had placed so low. The coach at the time, Lin Dunn, wanted to pick either Bird, Oklahoma's Stacey Dales, or North Carolina's Nikki Teasley.

"There was a lot of hype about the first pick, and a lot of people were saying it was going to be me," Bird said to *AP Online* right before the draft. "But what if it's not? I'm going to feel like an idiot."

CHAPTER FOUR

In the end, Dunn chose Bird. She would play alongside the previous year's number one draft pick, Lauren Jackson from Australia.

Almost as soon as Bird joined the Storm, the team began to turn around. On August 11, 2002, the Storm defeated Utah 74-57. That season, the team made it to the WNBA playoffs for the first time in **franchise** (FRAN-chyz) history. In 2004, the team won its first WNBA championship.

Also that year, Bird reached her childhood goal when she made the U.S. Olympic Women's Basketball team. Although she did not get to play much, she was thrilled to be part of a team that won gold at the Athens games.

She was even more thrilled when she was asked to play again in 2008—this time as one of the leaders of the team. The squad won all eight of its games in Beijing (bay-JING), and Bird won her second gold medal.

It was a very proud time for Bird. She told *The New York Times* that a college championship means the most to the fans

Bird sings the national anthem after the U.S. team won the Olympic gold medal in 2008.

of that school, and a WNBA championship is important to the fans in your team's city. Olympic teams, on the other hand, get support from the whole country.

"A certain respect comes from people who aren't even basketball fans when they hear that you're an Olympian," she said.

Bird joined the Russian women's basketball team Spartak Moscow in 2007. Overseas, she not only makes more money, but she also has free housing, a personal chef, and a driver.

Here and Abroad

Many WNBA players compete almost year round. They play from June to September in the United States. Then, in the winter, they play basketball overseas, for teams in countries such as Spain, Russia, Turkey, and Korea. In 2004, Bird joined the Russian team Dynamo Moscow.

It was very difficult for her to be so far away from her family. She thought about not returning to Russia for a second season. Then her college teammate, Diana Taurasi, decided to play there, so Bird joined her. In 2007, Bird and Taurasi played for Spartak Moscow.

By playing overseas, players gain experience—but they also earn a lot of money.

In the WNBA, players earned between $34,500 and $95,000 in 2010. (Men play in the NBA. The lowest-paid NBA player earned $473,604.) In Russia, Bird was paid about four times her Seattle Storm salary.

Since Bird joined the Storm, her team has had three different head coaches and three different owners. Only two players—Bird and Jackson—have been with the team since 2002. With all that change, it's no wonder Storm fans have been drawn to Bird. She is a competitive leader known for her **consistent** play. She is such a popular player that photos of her are used on billboards, buses, and buildings around the Seattle area.

The 2010 Storm team **dominated** (DAH-mih-nay-ted) the league with a 28-6 record during the regular season. The team won all 17 of its home games and every one of its **postseason** (POST-see-zen) games to win its second WNBA championship.

In the days after the 2010 playoffs, Storm coach Brian Agler praised his player. "Sue, to me, flies under the radar of getting

Bird drives past L.A. Sparks player Noelle Quinn during a 2009 matchup.

Bird makes a no-look pass around the Atlanta Dream's Coco Miller during the 2010 WNBA finals.

exposure [ek-SPOH-zhur]," he told the *Seattle Times*. "She does her job on the floor better than anybody."

Bird would be the first person to point out that a single player cannot make a team successful. Players must work well together, support each other, and trust each other. Still, her leadership and talent have helped turn the Seattle Storm into a basketball powerhouse.

In the words of former Storm coach Lin Dunn: "Our team got better when we started thinking about selecting Sue Bird."

Career Statistics

Year	Team	G	Min	FGM	3PM	FTM	REB	STL	BLK	TO	AST	PTS
2002	SEA	32	1,121	151	57	102	83	55	3	109	191	461
2003	SEA	34	1,136	155	49	61	113	48	1	110	221	420
2004	SEA	34	1,136	151	64	73	106	51	5	87	184	439
2005	SEA	30	1,020	130	45	59	72	29	6	87	176	364
2006	SEA	34	1,076	137	56	59	102	61	5	88	162	389
2007	SEA	29	919	118	45	22	57	43	8	67	143	303
2008	SEA	33	1,111	172	47	74	84	39	3	88	169	465
2009	SEA	31	1,101	154	54	35	78	47	3	81	179	397
2010	SEA	33	1,005	135	59	36	88	50	5	60	190	365
Career		290	9,625	1,303	476	521	783	423	39	777	1,615	3,603

(G = Games played, Min = Minutes played, FGM = Field goals made, 3PM = Three-pointers made, FTM = Free-throws made, REB = Rebounds, STL = Steals, BLK = Blocks, TO = Turnovers, AST = Assists, PTS=Points)

CHRONOLOGY

1980   Suzanne Brigit "Sue" Bird is born October 16 in Syosset, New York.

1998   Bird's high school team, Christ the King Regional High School, goes undefeated, wins the state championship, and is named national champion by *USA Today*. Bird earns a basketball scholarship to the University of Connecticut (UConn).

2000   Bird and her UConn teammates win the NCAA Division I basketball championship.

2002   As a senior, she leads her team to another NCAA championship, leads the nation in free throw shooting (94.2 percent), is named to the NCAA Final Four All-Tournament Team, and is honored as Best Female College Athlete at the Tenth Annual ESPY Awards. The Seattle Storm select Bird in the first overall pick of the WNBA Draft. She helps lead the Storm to their first playoff appearance. She is one of only two rookies to make the All-WNBA First Team.

2003   She becomes the third player in WNBA history to record more than 200 assists in a single season (221).

2004   She scores her 1,000th career point on June 22 and helps the Storm win its first WNBA Championship. She plays for the gold medal-winning U.S. Olympic women's basketball team in Athens, Greece. During the WNBA off-season, she joins the Russian team Dynamo Moscow.

2005   She hits her 200th three-pointer on July 23.

2006   She records her 2,000th career point on August 1 and is named to the WNBA's All-Decade Team. She continues to play for Dynamo Moscow, reaching the Russian championship and the EuroLeague women's playoffs.

2007   Bird has a successful operation on her injured knee. She is named to her fifth WNBA All-Star game but does not play because of her injury. She records her 1,000th career assist on July 1. In EuroLeague play, she joins Spartak Moscow in Russia, and they win the EuroLeague championship.

2008   She helps the U.S. Olympic women's basketball team win the gold medal in Beijing, China, then leads Spartak Moscow to both the Russian championship and its second EuroLeague championship.

2009   She is selected as a starter in the WNBA All-Star Game for the sixth time in her career. On July 17, she reaches 3,000 points in her career.

2010   The Storm captures a second WNBA Championship, winning every game they play in the postseason. Bird is named to the All-WNBA Second Team.

2011   In an ESPN pre-season poll, nearly 92 percent of general managers name Sue Bird the WNBA's best point guard.

FIND OUT MORE

Books

Berry, Skip. *Kids' Book of Basketball: Skills, Strategies, Equipment, and the Rules of the Game*. New York: Kensington Pub., 2002.

Bird, Sue, and Greg Brown. *Sue Bird: Be Yourself*. Kirkland, WA: Positively for Kids, 2004.

Shaller, Bob, and Dave Harnish. *The Everything Kids' Basketball Book: The All-Tme Greats, Legendary Teams, Today's Superstars – And Tips on Playing Like a Pro*. Avon, Massachusetts: Adams Media, 2009.

Works Consulted

Ackert, Kristie. "Bird Relishing Her School Days." *Daily News* [New York], March 31, 2002.

——. "With Bird, Uconn Flying High Again Hopes to Land in Final." *Daily News* [New York], March 30, 2001.

Bird, Sue. "Hero's Hero: My Sister, Jen Bird." The MY HERO Project. http://myhero.com

Bondy, Filip. "Sue Bird, U.S. Women's Olympic Basketball Team Ready to Fly." *Daily News* [New York], August 8, 2008.

Brewer, Jerry. "Brian Agler Can Attest: Sue Bird Is the Best of Her Kind." *Seattle Times*, September 17, 2010.

Caple, Jim. "Seattle Storm Guard Sue Bird Answers 10 Burning Questions with Page 2–ESPN." *ESPN: The Worldwide Leader In Sports*, June 25, 2009. http://sports.espn.go.com/espn/page2/story?page=bird/090623 &sportCat=wnba.go.com/espn/page2/story?page=bird/090623&sportC at=wnba

Elfman, Lois. "Globetrotting Sue Bird Makes Time for Home." *Syosset Patch* [New York], February 22, 2010. http://syosset.patch.com/articles/ globetrotting-sue-bird-makes-time-for-home

Evans, Jayda. "Storm Is Gearing Up for Another Title Run." *Seattle Times*, May 14, 2011.

Evening Magazine's "The Best of Western Washington and Northwest Escapes," 2010. http://best.king5.com/king-5-s-the-best/people/ friendliest-pro-athlete

McCauley, Janie. "Uconn's Bird Impresses Storm Owner." Online article. *AP Online*, 2002. www.highbeam.com/doc/1Pl-52428316.html

Smith, Michelle. "Sue Bird the Calm in Seattle Storm–NBA FanHouse." *NBA Team News, Scores, Standings, Schedules, Stats & Transactions*, September 11, 2010.

FIND OUT MORE

Terry, Mike. "It's Country First, Mate: WNBA's Lauren Jackson and Sue Bird Make Transition to Being Olympic Opponents." *Los Angeles Times*, August 3, 2004.

"WNBA General Managers Make Their Picks for 2011," *ESPN.com*, June 2011. http://www.wnba.com/features/gm_survey11_players.html

On the Internet

Euro Basketball League
http://www.eurobasket.com/?Women=1
The Seattle Storm
http://www.wnba.com/storm
Team USA
http://basketball.teamusa.org
The WNBA
http://www.wnba.com

GLOSSARY

AAU—Short for Amateur (AM-ih-chur) Athletic (ath-LEH-tik) Union (YOON-yun), this is the largest nonprofit sports organization in the United States. It supports athletic events and competitions in 34 different sports.

competitive (kum-PEH-tih-tiv)—Playing hard; taking a game or performance seriously.

confide (kun-FYD)—To trust with a secret.

consistent (kun-SIS-tunt)—Reliable or steady.

defender (dee-FEN-der)—A player whose main task is to keep the other team from scoring points.

dominate (DAH-mih-nayt)—To play on a higher level.

draft (Drahft)—The selection of players for professional sports teams.

exhibition (ek-seh-BIH-shun)—In sports, a game played for show, not to determine a team's standing.

exposure (ek-SPOH-zhur)—Media attention.

franchise (FRAN-chyz)—A professional sports team and the organization that allows it to operate.

hardwired (HARD-wyrd)—Naturally that way.

NCAA—The initials for National Collegiate (kuh-LEE-jit) Athletic (ath-LEH-tik) Association (uh-soh-shee-AY-shun); the league for college sports.

opponent (uh-POH-nunt)—An individual or team who competes against another in a game or contest.

postseason (POST-see-zen)—A time right after the regular season during which playoff games are held to find a champion.

rebounder (ree-BOWN-der)—A player who is skilled at getting the basketball after a missed shot.

tradition (trah-DIH-shun)—A long-held pattern of behavior or actions.

INDEX